MIRRORWORK

Also by Mimi Khalvati from Carcanet

In White Ink

Mimi Khalvati

MIRRORWORK

CARCANET

Acknowledgements

Acknowledgements are made to the editors of the following publications in which some of these poems have appeared:

As Girls Could Boast (Oscars Press 1994), *Bête Noire, Critical Quarterly, Leave To Stay* (Virago 1995), *Pivot* (USA), *PN Review, Poetry Review, Seam, Sheffield Thursday, Spadework, The Blue Nose Anthology* (Blue Nose Press 1993), *The Long Pale Corridor* (Bloodaxe Books 1995), *The North, Turret Books/Raymond Danowsky Broadsheets 1st series, Under The Asylum Tree* (Survivors' Press 1995), *Writing Women.*

I would like to thank The Arts Council of England for awarding me a Writer's Bursary for 1994.

First published in 1995 by
Carcanet Press Limited
402-406 Corn Exchange Buildings
Manchester M4 3BY

A CIP catalogue record for this book
is available from the British Library.
ISBN 1 85754 114 6

The publisher acknowledges financial assistance
from the Arts Council of England

Set in 10pt Garamond Simoncini by Bryan Williamson, Frome
Printed and bound in England by SRP Ltd, Exeter

FOR TOM

Contents

Mirrorwork

(for Archie)

Of course the serendipity of it moved me:
    a mirror-tree as metaphor become a
    mirror-tree as mural; a cherry outside
    my window become a willow in a tableau.
    The real become imaginal and vice versa.

Fooled me into forgetting, as I stopped just
    past the newsagent's on sunny days to
    see it glitter, how excitement, tempered
    by dismay, had first become, like the
    tree, asymmetrical.

Dismayed not so much that the willow-tree of
    England should deck itself in mirrorwork
    but that mirrorwork should lend itself to
    partwork, curvature, rising and falling
    as diadems of light on the willow's rise
    and fall, highlight, finite,

the inextricability of light and shade,
    infinitude of subject and reflection
    compromised by paint, ceramic, broken
    tile, glass used as decoration.

It marks the Silver Jubilee 1977. Below
    the roofline is captioned: THE ISLAND.
    I know nothing more about it. The area
    is still new to me but, as the mirror-
    tree seemed to suggest, somewhere to
    come home to, on my own terms.

You know all this, or some of it. Who
    never asked of me a poem, but a dedication.

You remember half the story: the mirror
  side that glitters. But the cherry-
  tree in Highgate fed through all those
  years with blank looks behind glass,
  my smoke, your smokescreens, silences
  disclaiming even argument – you forget
  how I gendered her, mirrored her.

She hangs my bedroom lights like globes
  against her throat, recycles snow as
  blossom when I am retrograde with
  childhood, still wearing winter clothes

and like a jaded lover levelling eyes across
  a road, cares little how I summer, what
  ornamental fruit I find to match her own.

I saw in her indifference yours. In her
  blossoms my bitterness at England. I
  never saw the cherry-tree. I'm not
  interested in trees. But in matching
  your indifference.

I refuse the natural detail to tell you how
  things look, how sky would look without a
  tree to blot my view of an avenue through
  cloudbanks like the genie from the bonfire
  growing longer, quieter, skyward.

Standing in its plot, its absence of a
    paving stone, my cherry-tree dissembles
    intimacy in echoes, seasons I think
    mirror me like the bric-a-brac of homes
    that took me in but were not mine

though I knew as well as they where biscuits,
    string or dog-lead lived and could be
    seen – by strangers walking past – at
    a dresser, drawer, brutally at home in
    the world as any back view in a window

or frontal view of cherry, dogged as a
    greeting card with yet another Eden,
    yet another plot of fruit, cat, bird.

You chose red for the bedroom carpet.
    How were you to know how much there
    was already in duvet, pillow, curtain,
    kimono? How was I to know, agreeing,
    the fights ahead?

Yearning for a metaphor to do what mother
    never did, lovers tried and failed,
    childhood sends its feelers out, finding
    dreams, clay figurines, to grub around,
    nose against.

Other nights it floods, dams burst open,
    sluice-gates slither rushing into
    blood, first blood: *My Queen is here!*

And tiles are floods of faeces, rooftops
    dropping into halls where aunts, like
    knights at an odd remove, appear in
    slants of light as though life were
    merely doubt and not disaster.

So childhood finds a cherry-tree, a tree
    of flimsy blossoms.

Feeds this tree through every fork with
    terrors, motherless.

See how it grows, canvasses for echoes,
    thunders with its tiny leaves, stops
    dead – as wind – in silence!

I've curtained off the tree today,
    pretending that her half of sky is
    greyer, wetter, more opaque. The
    half I see through, where no tree is,
    is lighter, actual.

My mother has gone on a coach trip with
    the Royal Academy and of course it's
    pouring down with rain. Her glasses,
    some days dark and some days clear,
    are pressed against a dream of heat
    behind the pane.

Beyond this cul-de-sac is a no man's land
    where a clutch of trees in shade, water
    in a bucket still rocking from the rhythm
    of a back that halts to stretch, droplets
    on a forearm shimmering with pinpoint suns,
    reclaim

energies of land, water, sun from scrutiny,
    assert their own economy, impervious as
    nature is to human dialogue and pain.

My tree is nothing but the thought of something
    not itself: a bare land that throws its
    own desire for shadow, orchard, rain.

What was that crow that came and went?
  Jagging a star like brick through glass
  first in blossom, now in air...

My mother on a coach trip, the Queen anointed
  in her golden coach stalwart in the heart
  of England, I in my room looking out through
  windows as gales of rain go past in light

crowd fractured dreams against the glass
  while rivulets outlast them, splayed
  like bony handprints on either side of
  faces we have worn, outworn, birthdays
  still tried on for size but never quite
  grown into, in the flurry and the hurry,
  our rows of fallen birds.

It is the bird on the one note stabbing the
  air that carries the morning.

I wait till dusk for someone else to tell me
  Live!

I used to look for you in books, divine you
in Susan Griffin's WOMAN AND NATURE, *find*
you in MATTER, SEPARATION (Where He Begins).

I'd close my eyes, place thumbs against the
first half (where I knew you were), will you
out of the margins of this strange I Ching.

Mathematician, archaeologist, astronomer,
something to do with husbandry, marquetry,
dressage, optics, you were all these things.
You spoke in number, weight, measure, myth,
from chambers, mooncraters, 'time itself,
gathering speed'. Your tools were bronze,
their points fine as pins.

Once in a blue moon you were soft and vul-
nerable, 'one hand awake even in sleep'.

'Foolish, crazy'? Perhaps. Seeing you
was always easier when you could have
no hand in it. Perhaps seeing you was
secondary. Never seeing you, lonely.
Or without the comma, and not never…

At no time does the private bond between
mind and mind speak with greater clarity
than when one loneliness speaks to another.

For days I've tried to trace its jagged
    outline in the air: the crow that came
    from nowhere, left its black impression,
    crowstar on my brain.

But each crowstar in this series – angled
    vacancies in space – is larger, vaguer than
    the one before, the first I saw, till today's.

Today's is the air itself: beyond these walls,
    ceiling, swollen to meet a force that has
    taken hold of angles, starpoints, streamed
    them into prayer ribbons whose aura I sit
    crowned in, like a hermit in a cavern,
    a ledger-clerk at some heavenly gate.

Opposite, the cherry-tree with its small
    grey gaps keeps scribbling across my sky
    while the crowstar gap that took the
    shock, black on white, has disappeared.
    Only the greys are left. I approach them.
    Through memories of crowstars, each held
    like a Qur'an above my head.

When sun promises a patch of sky bluer
    than the rest, I remember as a child
    looking up at sky, never seeing the
    legs around me, things tied to earth,

faces of carol singers, chapel readers
    oblivious to the company of angels.

Always above, beyond, were pathways of
    desire rising like lost balloons ever
    higher, higher. On an ottoman of cloud
    were no Gods, Kings, Olympians, but
    old men nonetheless, in cloth of gold
    with fruit and feast, ranged in a
    long, light wait.

Walking back from playing-fields with vows
    held like bonfire heat warm inside my
    blazer, I would then see, as if for
    the first time, figures round me,

alpines, flaking bark, and place myself,
    precise as any living thing, among them.

In every flower, blade or cloud I willed
    my longings into, is a memory of power,
    access to a short cut I can't name.

Where has it gone, the eye to eye, flank
    to flank, the same word of the same
    sentence said together, stopped together,
    unseeingness of arms around, eyes behind
    each other's backs?

A boy from Basra, numbed and being in a cell
    too dark to see, imagining that his arms
    had gone, kept asking where they had
    taken them, kept asking where we keep them.

Where, in a world we tear apart, a world
    we cannot share imagining that submitting
    to the test of glass and what we deem as
    glass we might see ourselves in him and
    him in us, might use our arms to hold him,
    touch his own and tell him...

But it's we who are in the dark. Unable
    to re-member the body that once believed
    it could not split and still survive,
    who cried to the child that broke its
    banks *Die, damn it, die! Let me survive!*
    and did, to say that this is Eden, this
    the body, fruit and snake.

We are the thought of something not itself.
    Each fragment whole, each unit split, but
    dovetailed, one wall, one dome, in whose
    muddied lakes of colour swim the blues
    of a bag, green rings of a skirt. We
    are the hall of mirrors, fine mosaic,
    the mirrorwork in which not even Kings
    can see themselves.

Yards from the mural, through the trees:
    glimmerings of silver, glints you might
    mistake for sunlight on a frontispiece,
    optical illusions.

Disclosed, willow branches bifurcate into
    angels' wings, epaulettes amassing,
    dripping silver.

Look up close: back into its splintered
    eyes! Retinas of leaf look back at you
    in unison. Living green in painted,
    living eyes in eye-slits. Voices
    thrown, disowned. Ventriloquism.

Tree in glass recoils from you, leans to
    orbit, stars. Shine without reflection.

A celebration. Faded to a fresco by
    breakage, refuse, accident. Pick one
    mosaic: crock from Turkey, blue on white,
    shop-surround in Ankara, Stoke Newington.

Hair of waterfall on brick, leaf-flèche, braid.
    There's no escaping silver. Mercury's
    plunge downwards. Running crests that
    leap: *The Great Wave off Kanazawa.*

A sea so bright with moonshine that it blinds
    its own horizon. Awed at the power of
    motion. The power of awe to still an ocean.

Under the green canopy are painted locals,
  mostly children, festive at a table.
  In geometrics – jellies, cakes, the usual
  bright concoctions. A photographer,
  black-suited, unnaturally large, with his
  right arm raised. Two boys with a spade.

CLEARING THE RUBBISH NOV 78, lettered on
  a wheelbarrow, stirs a memory of people
  who, catalogue to hand, captions, dates,
  stand in galleries and gardens asking
  factual questions, filling in the context.
  The English are good at this. Iranians
  hopeless.

Coming upon mirrorwork in Hackney, my father,
  for example, might shake his head (denoting
  in Iran admiration), note differences between
  theirs and ours – mirrorsmiths, community –
  and feel, without expressing it, a severance,
  a loss of context.

Around the corner, from behind his shop-window,
  the dry-cleaner waves to someone passing.
  No-one looks at the mirror-tree. It has
  grown on them, from birth for some, drained
  its dazzle into eyes grown tired of dazzle.

I glance as I pass. Not with indifference
  but an incipient sense of the customary.
  Seeing things as they are. You, me.
  Accommodating difference. On its own terms.

*

Vine-Leaves

Even the vine-leaves shot with sun
have shadow leaves
pressed close on them.

Even the vine is hanging
ones that seem like twos:
a top leaf
on a shadow leaf, its corner slipped,
like invoices in duplicate.

If I stood to look from the other side
with the light behind me,
would I still not see
how the top leaf shot with sun
might be the one that fails to fit
its duplicate

instead of
– standing where I do – seeing
how it is the shadow leaf that fails to fit
and failing

makes the one leaf seem like two
and being two, more beautiful?

Au Jardin du Luxembourg (detail)
after Henri Cross

If summer had its ghosts, gifts of wind
wind blows to you and whisks away,
then these two small girls

in pale pink flared
like two sweetpeas
I would take for mine and twirl them
to the balustrade...

Look how, squatting, peering down
they think the ground a river,
a winding in the gravel

whose underwater mysteries
like gaps between our memories
appear and disappear...

Like gaps between our memories
that reappear through tow-ropes
seemingly in reach, then, far out

where leaves are light
and light is fish
persuade us with a colour,
dissuade us with a depth

twirl them back through leaflitter,
parkland, crossroads, up and over
chimneystacks, birchsmoke, lavender

till, like gaps between our memories,
seed and dust and all wind carries,
they are seen at such a distance

we think them elemental
light, fire, air!

Coma

Mr Khalvati? Larger than life he was;
too large to die so they wired him up on a bed.
Small as a soul he is on the mountain ledge.

Lids gone thin as a babe's. If it's mist he sees
it's no mist he knows by name. *Can you hear me,*
Mr Khalvati? Larger than life he was

and the death he dies large as the hands that once
drowned mine and the salt of his laugh in the wave.
Small as a soul he is on the mountain ledge.

Can you squeeze my hand? (Ach! Where are the hands
I held so tight to pull me back to the baize?)
Mr Khalvati? Larger than life he was

with these outstretched hands that squeezing squeeze
thin air. Wired he is, tired he is and there,
small as a soul he is on the mountain ledge.

No nudging him out of the nest. No-one to help him
fall or fly, there's no coming back to the baize.
Mr Khalvati? Larger than life he was.
Small as a soul he is on the mountain ledge.

What Seemed so Quiet

when I listen hard
is bird to bird, wheel on rain,
what you say, I say.

How tall the pines are!
Heads thinned, as though to hear what
heaven says through wind.

The harder grey falls
the brighter grows the dream of
light, and wind (like rain

that is only heard
as it meets our world on water,
stone or pane), wind

itself a silent
thing you think would drown you out
well might, but also

carries you the more
to blow through open windows
like my own, in Highgate.

Sandpits

Sandpits from long ago sadden me.
I will give them topsoil, John Innes No 2,
bring them in like seedtrays, water them
from moon rivers springing even here,
trickling in a stream between my fingers.

What will grow? Miniature palms?
Poplars rustling in the ebb and flow
of shallow river-beds fed by snows
from Anatolia? Where two waters meet,
hedges rolled round turquoise pools? A pear?

I shall grow here; from patience, solitude,
vision old-fashioned as a cottage garden
that keeps a hold on history, a slower way
of doing things and pays the price by being
hard to get to, overlooked by motorways.

My own oasis; surrounded by what is sloughed,
grown into and grown out of: womb, clothes,
marriages and friends, and now, body,
losing elasticity, inch by inch
discarding me, as I do it, to self.

This shall be my birthplace; where nothing grows
for those who think to see a shoot, a tip,
a thin white stem that curls up like a question
only gardeners, head gardeners can answer.
A coffin then; earth you peer on, wondering

what death is like, where one goes, when you
yourself will go there. But I cannot rise
above my body, find answers in my self.
I, too, can only see this earth and somewhere,
not closeby, but hanging immanent in air

or in a taxi still weaving in and out of
traffic, the smell of marigolds eludes me.
The driver said he had bought ten pounds' worth
of marigolds that day and hours later,
still in their trays, had nothing left but stems.

I've been at it since 3 o'clock, he said,
putting plant pots out. They like to crawl
up inside where it's damp and muggy. The dustmen
won't be happy – they'll weigh a ton those bags.
Thousands upon thousands of live snails.

Have you got ivy? Funny you should say that.
I thought to myself just this afternoon
that's what it was. Perfect breeding place.
I've got ivy, too, I said and thought
of Jane, who told me off for killing snails.

She thought me heartless and I thought her amateur,
like a parent who only sees his kids on Sundays.
Yet we both love flowers. Love that can't be weighed.
Yes, sandpits sadden me...
And so, come to think of it, do seedtrays.

Deer Dreaming

Ten years of sweetness on a small scale, sleeping
on her father's jacket, my daughter's face,
her dreamface, is one window of a dreaming.
Scalds and sandhills, meanders and petroglyphs
have no bearing on this pastoral, bark
flashing signals on my eyelids. However,
two journey lines drive into me: a dream
with no horizon line, no body marking.

Facing backwards on a train with the landscape
drawing away from me, I travel only
a short route into its sadness, wire-fencing
distanced into aerial dots, deers' antlers
into stands of trees: a lost settlement,
a broken spirit galvanised to tracks
draining from the body through windows, windbreaks,
diverging into flatness, greyness, fields.

Deer make horrific noises when they mate;
wake you at night, to impotence and fists.
A baby in the carriage cries. A caged deer,
frantic, filthy, an enclosure, back garden:
another window of a dreaming. Stroked,
how it clung to me, rubbed my leg! Mucus
strained across my hand, how I rained those blows
on indifference, his face, hers, still sleeping!

They refused to take the doe back – pointblank –
back to where they took her from, to a time
they cared enough for deer to make her captive.
I wanted to be shot! of her. But violence
only woke me, to impersonate the deer
in me, or dear, not knowing what either means.
The meaning is not written, the disguise is.
The deer sits upright; wears its mask and munches.

Boy in a Photograph

The wind is up and as we
wind down it grows harder, colder, harsher.
He is the boy

arms around his knees
like a shepherd in a loincloth
dappled under trees

who gazed out to the hills
where life somewhere else raced faster.
His watchface even now

is skudding on his wrist,
tracking like a ninja-cloud
following its master. (The wind

was up but has changed its mind,
only leaves in close-up
are blowing harder...)

What was it he was gazing at
across those hills, eyes trained
on a flare, ears keened to a call

of horizons? We have captured him
and blown him up, in shade, in youth,
while his unseen flock

– what flock, what fleece? –
grows larger, smaller, larger.

The North-Facing Garden

(for Jill)

I have never seen her in the garden.
Never heard her gardening. Only heard her
talk of moonlight walks, perhaps tonight,
if the clouds clear.

I have seen her white carved girls, yawning
in a gentle stretch, outcrops where Himalayan
balsam drops its caramel in berries
loved by birds.

I have heard no-one in the garden.
Heard nothing but the waterfall, fountain,
the pitter-patter in steamrise, after rainfall,
that dribbles off at seven.

Yet someone must have gardened it. Hours
every day for years. The evidence is there –
barrow, cuttings, a ladder in the wood – someone
who did it all before we came.

Like the Indians before Columbus.
Like nature before woman stepped,
hair dripping like a seal, with her infant
out of water.

Or the invisible footmen of our childhoods,
shadow hands that served us, we
who were Beauty, at the table of the Beast
we also were.

Here, shadows are where colour grows
though only rose, all shades of rose
from the palest of anemone to dogwood, wedlock
or heard in hart's tongue fern.

The garden facing North takes its colour
not from sun but from her face: deepening
in the evenings, stove-flushed, lamplit, waking
to a bedroom facing West –

Why I'm no good in the mornings, she says.
Behind the eyes, smile, dip and rise of features
that apologise for the poverty of words,
stones speak, spirits prove

and with time on her hands, she makes Eden hers:
re-entering through a backdoor stone-propped open,
unseen behind an arch, hovering like a shade
of our former selves.

Writing in the Sun

is a kind of blindness:
blinded by the sun
and blinded in the shade

in a vague abstractedness to leaf
– like a library of words
heard dimly or forgotten –

writing in the sun
is what would make

re-entering a room
as cool, hushed,
as walking into sleep

if sleep were
a marble void
on the threshold of cathedrals.

For a moment it seemed easier
to walk towards the park
purposeless

than to take my life in hand,
become, if only for an instant,
someone writing in the sun

when one instant of imagining
walking into people's prayers
might be answered
with another and another.

Prayer

has nothing of the grandeur
or the violence of crowds
but circles stockinged
in its own quiet sphere

like lamplight sealing off what gloom sees
by its cone against the dark,
an interval when, weightless,

the body loses cut and thrust,
rises like a plume of smoke
to add its grievances to air's.

Prayer
is like watering the plants,
popping out to get the paper,
a trundling, pottering,

an audience for dust
that settles even as the duster's hand
moves across the grain.

Prayer can interrupt itself – fling
instructions over a shoulder, offer
delicacies on a shelf;

resume itself, its murmuring,
like berries, herbs
left drying in the sun

as, moving out of earshot,
you find your own momentum,
your freedom not to pray.

Prayer is not a scourge.
Though the head bows, back stoops,
it is a lifting, a soft and drifting
spiral like the echoes of a string plucked,

a sky to feel alone in,
how small one is, how packed
the earth with people;

how far the neighbour's radio
– as skin meets stone – recedes
and amber beads count amber suns
that are still to rise, still to set.

Prayer is a time of day
that, on a winding stair,
greets itself.

Interiors

after Edouard Vuillard

Edouard Vuillard (1868-1940) lived with his mother until her
death when he was 50. Mme Vuillard was a seamstress and her
workroom, like his studio, was part of the home. 'The home and
the studio were one, and the honour of the home and the honour
of the studio the same honour. What resulted? Everything was a
rhythm, a rite and a ceremony from the moment of rising.
Everything was a sacred event...' (Charles Péguy, *l'Argent*).

My own mother was a dressmaker and my grandmother (who
bears some resemblance to Mme Vuillard!) presided over daily
visits to her home by seamstresses. This poem is intended as a
tribute, not only to Vuillard's art, but to the art of these women.

In many of the childhood *Studies*, I have tried to speak, in a
collective voice, not as 'the child within the adult' but as 'the adult
within the child'.

Much material is drawn from *Vuillard, His Life And Work* by
Claude Roger Marx (Paul Elek 1946), to whom I am indebted.

I   *Four Interiors*

THE PARLOUR

Between the saucer and the lip,
the needle and the cloth,
the closing of a cupboard door
and the reassertion of a room,

in those pauses of the eye
when the head lifts and time stands still

what gesture flees its epoch
to evoke a crowded continent?
What household conjures household

in the heterogeneity of furniture,
rituals that find their choirs
in morning light, evening lamps,
in cloths and clothes and screens?

This woman sewing,
man reading at his desk,
in raising eyes towards the wall
do they lose themselves in foliage?

Sense themselves receding
to become presences on gravel paths
and, in becoming incorporeal,
free to be transposed?

Do they see themselves and not themselves
– have any sense how manifold
might be their incarnations –
in the needlepoint of walls and skies
so distant from their own?

For this profile hazed
against shutterfold and sky
has as many claimants
as there are flowers on the wall,
in a vase, on a dress, in the air

and everywhere, like leaves,
recognitions drop their calling-cards
on a mood, a table set for supper,

disperse themselves as freely
as the mille-fleurs from a palette,

settle unobtrusively
as her to her sewing, him to his book,
lowering eyes from vistas
that have brought them to themselves.

THE WORKROOM

It was in the whirring of a treadle,
biting of a thread,
in the resumption of the treadle

while eyes were closed
and shadows of the scissors
like the noon sun through its zenith
were passing overhead

that allegiances were fed their rhythms,
loyalties first given shape.

With a lever sprung, a length released,
launched in its wake on a sea of stuffs,
flecks of wool, waves of walnut grain,

receiving food, receiving drink, we gave
the thanks we never knew in time
we would strive to give, to keep alive
in words, in songs, in paint.

It was in these gestures, the day's devotions,
with a pockmarked thumb, pinheads
jammed in a mouth that held them safe,
that an inheritance was slowly stitched,

a paradigm to give body to
like a second life to curtains,
a lining to a dress. And now,
when prayers we never knew were prayers

in the guise of silver bobbins,
machines we never mastered,
are once again in currency
in the hands of daughters making light

of the partnering, unpartnering of threads;
when voices caught, then thought lost
in transit while ours, in vows,
were still keeping faith

return in transpositions,
in a dream like a revelation,
familial as they were in life
to orchestrate our states of grace;

how can we not fail them?
What sacraments can we find but these
poor leavings of a memory
of a home, a time, a place?

THE STUDIO

Moving into an attic with skylights
that reflect
this attic, skylight,

this self-portrait that rises
from refuse round an easel,
refuse round a mirror, concretions
of a life fallen from the body,

concrete images by which we thought
to reconstruct our layers;

caught in an upper angle,
the triad by which light
consecrates mirror, wall,
the forehead's lobe

– a tightening of tension
between sky and thought
and where thought falls –
with an instrument at hand and memory
transfiguring, holding up prefigurements

of all the hand creates . . .
we move into a chain, a series of removes
like dinner guests at table recessive
in glass, like the painting of a painting
retracted to a sketch.

With skylight overhead
where birds divide their paths and cleave
its compass point as cleanly
as leaves cleave stems

or with fielded gold below
in those voids for interleaving,
becoming, ceasing,

and sounds of playing children
too far to be intrusive
like seabirds in a bay,

we are complicit in a subterfuge,
this series of removes,
diminutions to a dot

but cannot lose, nor even
drown in the grand design, that moment
when the eye lifts, the hand descends
to a description of itself.

THE BEDROOM

Sewing at her window,
leaning her head on a plane of light
like a cheek against its pillow

or watering her hyacinths,
whatever was passing through her mind
light from the lamp recorded,
light from the window guessed.

The room she had come to tidy,
tidied and left alone, embroidered it;
the air outside with its hooves and bells
indoors almost mute

spread it to thin in squares and parks
while flowers downstairs
on divans and chairs
rumoured it back to borders
flowering at her nape.

In doors always left half-open
she is suspended in mid-sentence

like a thought
too generous to express.

Entering, exiting
as part of the same slow motion,
gliding profiled to the right,
older, to the left,

hers are the two stooped figures
behind the scrim of childhood,
parentheses we are caught between,
stalled in their vague arcades.

Might they not be our muses?
Our covenants with absence?
Greys that are never storm and cloud
but oyster, dove and snail?

Might they be spelling a secret,
in codicils a condition:
if art is to nail a butterfly's wings
and a prayer for flight be the nail...?

If only it were a question of will!
But will, mourning our own mortality,
forfeits the gift of pity
art earns in mourning theirs.

II *Studies for the Workroom*

With an arm along a table,
a head against an arm
and the sensation of an eye

from the highest corner of the room
that looks down, sees only

our right side laid
in falls of light
while shadows on its underside
pulsate against an ear,

how childhood in its timelessness
like a fishspine between sun and moon

in this laying out of halves,
this pool of concentricity,
luxuriates!

And though the head stays still
while the mind, listing against currents,
logs driftwood on its way,

on frequencies faint
as lilacs in a beige

is such a weightlessness of objects,
scumbling of their outlines
that volition, like a craft

fazed by would-be voyagers
– colours and their offspring,
rhythms and their cargo –

is arrested at the rivermouth
while on the deck the masts,
long antennae of a daydream,

frame a stillness that might pass
for idleness.

While journeys made, or broached,
are left hanging in their harbours,
left hanging in farewells,

journeys daydreams sail on
surprise themselves with atolls:
an atoll in an Indian ocean

where birds that have lost their power of flight
because they have no enemies

make scissor-runs across sand and tide –
poignant, being flightless,
more poignant, being safe.

The eye is on us.
The eye is on a vertical
from the oilstove to the cornice,
ground floor to the upper,

lamp-post to the clouds –
anywhere we might be seen:
a shop, a park, a bed.

Seeing with neutrality
that small of a back, nape of neck
our familiars seem forgotten in

it rouses us to run to them,
wrap arms around the waist,
kiss the neck bowed over work,
have them turn to face the light

for where light strikes
the eye sees only
face or hands or hair.

Water makes things dark
but in the sprinkling bowl
it's red – a different red
from the bowl itself, yet red.

High on the mount of Venus,
on the flowering bulb where the thumb
still flowers,
a vesica once opened up

a bloodshot eye that cried
in blood, sweet melon-blood
it took hours of holding high,
of pressing hard, to stem.

Now closed in a thumbnail
scar, tiny scar inspected
on the train of red,

like an eyelid seeing inwardly
or a sickle moon
from its vantage, detachedly

it poses as a palmline,
records as any palmline would
how small the threat to life was,
how near the knife the vein.

The lever of the Singer
is a long slick thumb:

like saintliness
stern
on its own small world.

Under a human thumb pocked
not in rounds but triangles
of vanished skin like sails,

it sets the eye in motion:
level with an upper world,
a lower world, whether

an empty eye,
threaded eye,

eye that sees no difference
between function and futility,
action and mimicry, riding

gaily on its open plot,
its silver pole, its carousel.

Through flowerstems in water
drawing vowel-sounds of ghosts,

cousins' voices
drifting out of space,
through liquid slugging into jugs

and the smell of olive oil
– tomato pips like frogspawn
pooled on small glass plates –

comes the punctuation of a reverie,
a summons arcing over chairs.

A disc of air, bright or warm
to walk towards

forms when they call one's name.

But where, among figures stooping, stretching,
in tigerstripes and polka-dots,
working, sewing, sweeping,

women flattened into vase-shapes,
the ins and outs of drapes,

women always floor-length
whose elbows might be objects,
profiles air,

where, in a play of particles
is the figure centre-stage,
actor with his laughlines,
cardinal with crucefix,

the great divide
from which all distances, certainties
irradiate?

Here are two heads at an angle,
one woman cutting cloth
and both heads at an angle that suggests

an intimacy, rapport,
a solicitude

but may only be the one
from which
they see straight.

Drops of sweat fall on lawn, go grey
and white again under the iron's nose
as steam clears.

It clears on fields,
sewn one to another,
braided with a hedge.

On the far side of the hedge
is nothing:
no life except one's own,
the sky's, the trees', the clouds',

nothing where ought to be
the promise that was given
when one thought of looking there.

Tacking in an armhole
flashes semaphore and sunray.

Out in the park it is lighter
than it was, lighter than expected
as though the afternoon
reversed itself.

But here indoors, we're solid
as clocktime, any segment of a day,
any going in and out of rooms
that hold each other's voices
on the measures of a thread.

Over doorsills, tiles,
from the intensity of borders
to the middle ground and back again,
taking carpets at their own speed,
we move along their pathways;

even in the circle measured
to our own span, not alone.
Even when tonight, in our room,
voices silent in the thick of walls
talk among themselves, we will feel,

lodged long before we enter,
like a bass note to the moonlight,
a memory forgotten that will not go away,

the ceiling of a presence,
a company, a solitude,

like hearing in the dark
intermittent rain.

Under an eye that casts its threads
we duck, we weave, we cast our own

marking time until, on growing points
of verticals, that height is reached
from which

an eye might think it reasonable
to negotiate,
from which an arm might reach
to adjust the shutter gates

so that light pours down in a wider
sphere for those who now, penumbral,
taking up such little space,
weigh only lightly on the earth

to extend their own threads in,
their yards of worn elastic,
tethering ropes of sun and moon
between

the basin and the yard,
treadle and corridor,
conception and flowering –

anywhere they need to reach
with slack to spare.

Once the wheel is turned,
articulations of the lever
folded under cover for the night

and the need for counting stops
as blankets open up their triangles,
tartan rugs their squares,

those whose closing eyes rely
on an eye that keeps its vigil,
empowered in the dark to see
brighter in their stead, know,

relinquishing without resentment
their weight beneath its power,
how darkness can illumine

what day hid, life hid, to eyes
that grow accustomed to its glare.

III *Studies for the Parlour*

In the play of parallels, sightlines
reminiscent of a child's
cut off above, below
borders, banisters, picture-rails

are the verticals of harmonies,
horizontals of melody and inbetween,
where the ground shows through
in florals, filigree,

fleshtones
that are merely space for the eye to skim
or inadvertently alight upon

as a bird between two chimney pots
in the breaks between foliage,

as a life between polarities
now here, now there.

As the ear is to the orchestration
of sounds near and far, mingling, overlaid,

an orchestra in which the human voice
is an accent as a bird's is, the ring
of cutlery on glass, trowel on brick,

so, too, the eye,
seeing wallpaper as fabric,
a baby's cheek as millboard,
a butterfly
large and white above a path
that turns out to be a passerby
receding down a lane,

is, to the hierarchies of vision, blind
but, by some law of mimetism
able to convey

not only sounds and tastes and smells
but the workings of memory itself,
short-circuiting, choosing what it will

to light on, without a thought
for boundaries, vocabularies
that distinguish the substances
our world and we are made of,
landscape from the flesh.

Inside seams, colours never fade;
they have the heartlessness of furnishings
that have never known the wear and tear
of sunrise, sunset.

Feet phantom under hemlines know
no depths, wandering bodiless in rooms
where a girl is first the blue,
blue shape she represents.

The process of perception
– squandering of time, elasticity
of space – is all we recollect
of detail we once drowned in:

its anchorage so strong, faint,
luminosity so near the edge
as we dizzied off to galaxies
through the exactitude of parts –

left their workings in the pulse
of a flowerface.

Counting beads, apple pips, tiny things
only we are small enough to count on
– investments they know nothing of
in their indulgence of our games –

or colours by their nuances
stained, fatigued, in sun-leached lengths
reds no longer red;

turning marbles to the light
and marking indentations, the surface
scratch that tells us where we are
and were before is still the same,

we hold tomorrows solid in the promise
of growing powers, days to come
when pips give way to orchards –
apple-green, prune-violet, gooseberry-red.

Little do we dream, though,
that larger minds at ease
with magnitude, expansion,

will be as nonplussed as we are
by the small become dimensionless,
the infinite nonsensical,
by particles as fuzzy

as the kitten in the parlour
collapsing like a star
as it turns to catch its tail.

In the run behind the piano
where a pencil fell,

fluff collects, spiders die
and lead, having long ago
lost a train of thought or the point
of a calculation,

finds itself accepted
by a community of objects
oblivious of our own

in which the human element
is as leaf is to the branch,
pencil to the page.

Who is in the room then? Behind us
as we gaze into the mantelpiece, glass
behind the mantelpiece, seeing

the smoky backs of daisies, cards
that curl away from us, from unexpected
angles the closures of a room distorted
by dimensions meeting, repeating,
rising up their gradients, redefining

not who we are but the space
we thought familiar, the room
inside the drapes?

Do not turn round.
Count the petals of the daisy.
Between three and four, seven and eight,
sense

who passes in the corridor, enters
on their slippered feet and tidying up
not only cloth but vibrations that
might betray their wake,

folds the angle they have entered,
the hidden diptych in the corner
and, with linen on their arm, leaves you
to the daisy, the backward writing
in the mirror, pollen on the marble
you will smell but not disturb.

Caught between desire
to enter sitting-rooms illicitly,
huge among the ornaments, chairs
we dare not sit on in the presence
of the air's thin wraiths

and the line of least resistance
to rooms we have the run of
among the largenesses of elders,
whose bustling is our luxury,
our leave to be ignored in,

we hover on a landing
between the handle and the stairs:

for stowed away with odours, whispers,
mirrors where the souls of those we love
are skyed like chandeliers,

dimensions we know nothing of
– of lives played out before ours began,
games too human or too pitiable
to let us see, with the same eyes,
the world we saw this morning –

will lure us in with stories,
feed our hunger for the evidence
of crimes we cannot name.

Sauntering back through doorways then,
with an innocence no sooner lost
than reassumed, we take our place
at table, lift our eyes to faces

knowing nothing of our loss
but betraying, for the first time, theirs.

These were rooms
we should not have entered;
or entering, not taken fright,
fright at their premonitions,

the story with one ending
we would fight against
and in fighting

corrupt the spirit
that is outside the scope of stories
or is the one that has no end.

Behind every keepsake we touch or wonder at
through glass, is a world curtailed,
a household lost to history, a darkened room

where youths betrayed mark time
till they can reinhabit bodies
strewn again with roses,

be claimed again as integral
by the parenthood of death: deaths
that will leave these sitting-rooms
for us to light, too late.

It is now that we want them lit.
Now that we need the dancing. Now,
while a rosebud framed in a cream
of skin, black velvet on a neck,

little dreams in its dreams of dancing
of lives lived at such a distance
to those dreams as our dreams now

are to this life lived,
these daisy chains, thumbnail slots,
this small wild life that we ourselves curtailed.

Take a theme, an object near at hand,
near to heart and hand
and play it over again.

Each successive time you play
within it will be
the last time that you played it

and in this dialogue between the last
and the one before or after
your contribution, your part
in how a century sees itself.

Take a motif from a carpet,
the intimacy that kneels
at the foot of something larger,
too large to fit the frame

and again repeat it till,
flake by flake, glance by glance,
you have a covering of a corner

majesty throws light on
and, by reflection,
becomes aware of the concept of itself.

Though morning light and evening light
come, like echoes, friable as gunfire

and faith, in a weakening tug-of-war
between the reality that bombards us
and the will to give a body
to the latency inside us, wilts,

the memory of tables
vibrant with refracted light,
objects now forgotten
on their plastics or chenilles,

the child cluttering up the doorway,
the hand that eased her in,

the evocation of a lived-in grace
that continues to sustain us
however gracelessly we live

still connect with a source of love,
that sudden shining open space
to which words, conjoining as they near,
float in.

It was those glass-sprigged afternoons
the best part of us was born in.

Now, in a fading light – condensation
rising on the panes, snowing us in –
through a veil of milk

it aches, it glows, it passes...

*

Needlework

Within the lamplight's radius,
within the frame the flowers,
my name within my lifetime
handed on to no-one dies with me.

My knots are neat.
My cottage gardens will be stretched
with the ones my daughters stitch.
My youngest keeps me company.

On an upper landing where my work
is hung, in another century,
some strange and foreign woman
may try to picture me

and fail. Or is that I fail
to picture her? I cannot think
what she would want with me.
With hollyhocks and bonnets.

That Night, at the Jazz Café

everything about her was beautiful:
skin and hair and eyes proving
clichés holding true.

Was it fluorescence on her cheekbones,
kohl that made her eyes shine, silver
on a thong against her throat

or something in the way she held me
as though no skin or hair or bone
could ever come between us

that made her
– lovely as she'd always been –
that night, so much, much more?

No lover I, to name my love a rose!
No nightingale, old feather-dustered,
grey one I, in my daughter's cast-off clothes.

But if I were
I'd wing it to some stained-glass aisle
and, trapped between two musty shelves,

take my feathers to the dust
on gilt-edged tomes; then as paeans rose
from powdery skins, showered in a firefly fall

I too would throw my lot in, give vent
to the songs heard no more in a world
– God keep her safe –

in a world so pleased with its own distaste
what head would lift, librarian stop
for the nightingale and rose?

On Reading Rumi

Earlier, to be ready, I hoovered the carpet.
Fluff from your socks has strewn it like cotton-flowers.
I pick them, spin them to thread between my fingers.
Short threads. Where are you now?

Night is not the death of day. It is
her lying-in, her waters breaking. Why
not stay then? Ease her way? A new day,
stillborn, will only multiply our miseries.

Night, so you let us sleep *like fish in black water*!
Sluggish, I slow-nibble, stare. When I move,
my Master's line moves with me. Far above,
he is sleeping like a rock; too drunk to stir.

If, as you say, when I feel my *lips becoming
infinite and sweet*, when I feel *that spaciousness inside,
Shams of Tabriz will be there too*, please tell him,
graciously, two is company, three's a crowd.

My friend has broken up with her own friend –
and he's no Guide, whose lines might make amends.
If guidelines could, I'd give her, as a token –
the egg is whole, though the shell be broken.

Why should I listen when skin is more persuasive?
Or touch, when looking without touching can give
a taste of love so unlooked for, and so rare?
Today, your scent. Gratefulness rises on the air.

(Quotations are from *Quatrains of Rumi, Unseen Rain*, translated by John Moyne &
Coleman Barks)

Geraniums

The geraniums are still alive, and fuchsia;
lobelia, daisies ready to uproot
and in Tom's room
dwarf nasturtiums trumpet up a red
borrowed from some other flower
while one brass-orange hangs its head.

They do well here facing South whereas
those I saw trailing from the top floor
as I came back home
in my absence have been on a green rampage.

It's twilight in the kitchen – rather
twilight between the leaves outside,
a light grey over the dark of slates.
Gold inside the kitchen – an anniversary
kind of gold though none and none with whom
to celebrate.

I'm eating proper meals now, the fridge
is full of yoghurt, melon, raspberries,
I've even bought a plastic box for fetta,
at the same time strew
books, papers, clothes anywhere I like
for the luxury of meeting them as I might
the self I was two hours ago, later.

Twilight deepens: geraniums' red
fluorescent, fuchsia's tiny buds
running their pink down leggy stems –
buds unlikely now to open. September.

The window is a mass of leaves in
silhouette and the window-box, so bright,
so lit, almost a part of the room, itself
part of the night outside, one open door,
reflected, open to another.
I too am both in and out. In glass,
like an Indian movie star fronted
by geraniums. Indoors, smoking,
looking at flowers, the me my children
love me for, letting them go, still loving them.

Love

When someone sits on your bed
and strokes your hair for a long while
then quietly leaves,

though you feel the mattress
relinquish weight that anchored you
and float unsafe on a surface

that is even but seems to tilt,
though you hear him go, your loyalty
is now less to love than to night and day

whose death and resurrection
you are made
implicit in.

The Deer's Eye

is not an eye for seeing with;
mahogany, smoked glass, globed
wing mirror that inflects

a world of sound, scent, measures
the speed of flight against a veld,
the deer's eye is unchanging:

a spirit-lamp that does not guide
but follows where the will goes,
its level never changing

not even in a flat-out run
slow-motion disentangles into
splits, vaulted, folded,

or at dusk when those two lamps burn
as sight fades, dawn when they catch
the limb of a gibbous moon,

obscuring, reflecting
or radiant to the point
flame dies, light implodes.

To bring the deer's eye level
with your own, across bedclothes, nightroom,
like a newsreel, thriller,

brings you where you should not be:
unbeliever in a temple, voyeur
in a playground, armed, defended

in an arena where fight/flight
is a bolt through grass, judder
of a shin, gold of an eye with a pupil,

dark of an eye without,
its intelligence within.
To cheat this eye, steal from it

– be it with awe, tenderness –
intimacy, sensation, the right
to draw our metaphors,

superimpose, magnified, our vision
on an eye that cannot see
its own death filmed, is to justify

lives we cannot change,
lives that, left unchanged,
themselves change nothing.

Reaching the Midway Mark

reaching, for some reason, out for it
only to wake in a darkened room
where chair and clothes and bed

have no more weight than air has
in the daytime when all these things
are solid...mother, tell me.

Poet-mother, born of another
generation speaking through its own
veil, have you told me? I cannot find it.
Not the marrow, not the heart of it.
Is it

like daring to fill a room with light
when the house is dark...

how silence thins...
how sounds rush through in a sudden flood
but nothing breaks, not one thin strand
of silk? Is it

like prising open a fruit to find
torn ligatures of strawberry? Blue,

a blue that goes with Egyptian gold,
the bluest of blues the minute before
night thins itself with morning? Heavy,

disembodied? How the first time feels
when you ask a man *can I kiss you*, is it
how day and night change places?
To do with articles of clothing?
All the things I could tell you mother?
All the things they tell me.

The Face

Apart from – under the line of the eyebrow –
a line of olive swelling as an olive swells
to a glint of cream, two round black eyes
like two black cherries and those two plucked lines

surprised to find themselves so high above her eyes
no dialogue takes place
in all that space left in between,

nothing, as you pass her in the street,
of her face remains

except a certain light, a clarity,
a reflection not of sun or cloud
but of an image of desire,

an image of becoming
she has placed like God in sky
and though she thinks it private, preceding her
like sun, cloud, clear to any passerby

it pours across her face, unwritten, bare,
the force of all those futures
we have in mind, had in mind
and some we failed, some we now embody:

not an inner light, not an outer
though the sky glares and her face
is turned towards the place the sun should be

(and yours towards the station
with the light behind your back where motorways
span farmland, ring roads, open country)

but on her skin, an emptiness that glows
the way an empty morning
clarifies to an urgency, an image

whose name or face you do not know
but feel its tug, its urgent wish
to meet itself on paper
and by being seen, by seeing warn

the emptiness so filled with light, dream, hope
it cannot know
the worlds between

the beacon and the lines
that will get written
as they did on mine
on a face that passes in the street.

Christopher on Foot

Stepping out of his poems and into his
prose, is it freedom he steps into,
a kind of travelling on foot

where once he covered desert, tundra,
aerial views, now slowing by a verge?
Or something he steps out of –

not a suit of clothes, habits,
stanzas and modesties, but
out of the very thought-before,

its cartography, history, even
its family members?
Whatever it is – in reach now –

let there be no early frost,
boundary, no sign that points
the one way back;

let no-one spy on it, pull
or push at it, let it not be
tended brutally, impassively

but escape him, keep its distance
beckoning while he, hot and laughing
struggles, stumbles to keep track!

Apology

Humming your Nocturne on the Circle Line,
unlike the piano, running out of breath

I've been writing you out of my life
my loves (one out, one in).

I've pushed you out of the way to see
what the gaps in my life might look like,

how large they are,
how quickly I could write them in;

and not (at least till I've lost you both)
rewriting you only means

that the spaces I'm not writing in are where
I live.

A View of Courtyards

As though a courtyard were the pedestal
of a column – set in stone –
of air and sunmotes, winter draughts
that, ambushed in its paths of light,
struck canopies and eaves
with gloom, with gold...

as though cornices and lintels,
                parapets, window-jambs
etching shadow-teeth on terraces,
                    skiagraphs on brick,
were starclocks, sundials,
henges that were homes...

the way herdsmen move from slope to slope,
swallows wing from shelf to shelf

at the equinox they moved
lugging bedding, bundles, samovars
across the yard, past the pond
(holding heatwave safe behind their backs,
sunlight warm along their laps)
as the season turned
and the weaver's shadow
altered on the loom.

As sunrise spins itself in barberries,
dusk conceals in jams,
so kitchens faced the east
(for morning sun is good sun),
storerooms west
and in between, bicameral as the heart,
living room
.changed hands.

My lover phones to say he's had enough of this
– this never knowing what the time is –
and has bought himself two clocks.

North and south still chiming in my head
the bond between us tightens

and here we are again – though miles apart –
bound in our parallels, as he sets
bells ringing, times
a coincidence of paths.

As though sherbert vials, waterjars
were to think of dust, downtown,
roads going south where the Gulf lies,
vacant, under defunct oil-rigs

(where the urchin's light green eyes
are of thinnest glass, frontages
only fronds could ever wave behind,
no homefire burn in...)

and the insistent phrase
in search of its outlet song
could not escape so wide a plain
or the flute breath's holding,

undoing what damage the old view did
I place myself at thresholds
                    – vernal, autumnal –

garden
where my heart is.

But – paths running parallel – solstice
came and with it another separation,
so I brought the garden table in,
wiped web and rust, lined it up
with a sill whose outer half,
dark in the shade of a rampant vine,
will later catch its raisins . . .

Seldom used it. Used
the stones of my yard so well
– lying under lavatera – they buckle
even more now, splinter, tip dangerously
on the very step where my mother fell,
fractured her pelvis – first
in a line of hairline cracks
becoming broken cradles . . .

Moved back in. To my old desk,
an upstairs view of the Archway Road,
next door's rose failing to get a grip
on lace, across the road, my neighbours.

Having lost the power to move at will,
not my own, but the seasons',
encumbered with belongings
as though fixtures and fittings
were my metaphor for roots,
I function where my habit is

far from rooms determined
by the gold along a wall,
the alchemy of ponds
turning memory of water
to ice and back to water,

tied as I am by fear of loneliness to a man
whose contract with mobility
has shunted me off flightpaths,
passed me like a caravan.

Lacking southern sun
to leak from an unseen source
behind thicket, cloud or cornstack,
light to make it finite,

my shadow
is all ground on which I walk,
sky to which I turn,
no Mecca, no Jerusalem,

no weft or warp
in brickwork or basketry

to say I am, am not, I am.

Facing the Archway Road,
an older lifeline teases, thin
as a single hair but strong as fishing-line,
something going backwards
on an airpath between spine and door,
door and newel-post, that curlicues
the stairwell, exits into garden,
frazzles loose ends into air
that will snare them in illuminations,
the machinations of the zodiac.

Now love and light stored up in me
coincide with what went before,
before I lost my bearings,
coincidence of earth and sky,
past and future sibling grain
in our elders' sifting hands.

For divisions we have come to prise,
earth a house and garden we inhabit,
sky a bafflement of maths
despite moonwalks, space probes, sky labs,
they did not: saw themselves as underbelly
and sky a slender frame like Knut,
lid for sarcophagus and land.

As though an *eyvan*, meeting-point
of greeting, parting, verandah boards
over which a household trudged
or came to rest while an infant slept

were the locus of the soul
between the spirit that is garden,
body that is home

(where leg-bindings loosed
even as a journey ended
would let the heart go out,
the soul repair...)

I undress walls, pull
carpets back and forth
to redefine the focal point,

stoop to pick up mail.

Bedrooms were no battlefields,
no single parents' boxed retreats.
'Don't let the child sleep by herself!'
                              the women warned
as though night were a stranger offering sweets.

But night was a sling of bedrolls
                        flung this way, that way,
on terraces or carpets, wherever day had landed
childfalls, summer-calling cousins,
a bridegroom from the city

and bedrooms only latitudes
to give them bed and board
with every night a new – however fabulous –
configuration, ever redefining
what yesterday found fitting.

As for dining-rooms?
There was no such thing.
A tent, perhaps, in the orchard
of a house where you spent long summers,
remembered best its boiling vat,
globe of morning milk;

or the cooling length of a hallway
where the barest draughts slinked
in and out, reared at the door
as the cloth flared up
and rice came steaming in.

Spines that reached with ease for bread,
even the old, crosslegged,
thighbones lying flat on earth,
hipjoints opening down to earth
as though to help her
take them in.

As though, on some dazzling noon verandah,
an oil-lamp flame were left, like Cinderella,
still burning in its rags

every year the stars rise later,
emerge in half-light
when one's relation to the half-seen plants,
marrow under giant leaves, seems sacrosanct.

In a summer-house of six rooms,
in every room a fireplace, my mother
as a child scissored to their covings
cardboard floors, walls, interiors

she furnished with matchboxes, wire,
seashells, felt scraps; even
tiny rugs that bore, like exports,
the weave of a small girl's hand.

When inhabitants of the real rooms,
curling up on mattresses, in moments
before sleep, let their eyes fall
on sofas, bureaux, bedroom suites
any western home might have

it must have been as though
falling through a looking-glass
into daughters' lives where fires burn,
wood gleams, bedrooms where in every
nook and cranny is a turning in cocoons,
a learning and unlearning –

the past a cold stone fireplace,
oil-lamp with no wick,
journey into sand...

as though a doll's house with no dolls,
a dome within a dome
could have prophesied a shrinking world
where the soul mistakes
its yearning for migration
for freedom to cover earth's span;

even while furniture is being placed,
carpets tacked and the saw, screw,
unpartnering our seasons,
nailing down the flux,
the vagary of maps.

As though this loss, this giving away
of the shirt off one's back, discarding
a love that no longer fits

were only a pupal stage
and this flick of the pink, fireflash,
only fright colouration
before the moth takes wing,

with a click of the latch
I take to the bark,
fly my colours,

survive
on homegrounds wings can match.

Ham- is a Persian prefix meaning -mate,
so *hambazi* is a playmate,
hamclassi a classmate
and our word for neighbour
is *hamsayeh*, meaning
one who lives in the same shadow,
a shadow-mate.

A good word
is as a good tree –
its root set firm,
and its branches in heaven;
giving its fruit at every season
by the leave of its Lord.

I wish to learn the good words
in Gur'an or Bible,
in women's words or man's.

I wish to find their offspring,
the shadow-groupings in the fireplace,
this family or that *fameel,*
madar, pedar, dokhtar.

Learn how to set the future
newly-bathed upon my lap,
bring sky down to wrap us in,
feel myself as human as I am.

Have David at his desk across the street,
Karen in her kitchen
feel as close as fist to fist on rope
or gazing up the starclock chute
as the tug on heel and hand.

Have skylight be to calendar
what soul should be to self

vision
to these small repeated acts.